GRAPHIC NATURAL DISASTERS
EARTHQUAKES

by Rob Shone

illustrated by Nick Spender

FRANKLIN WATTS
LONDON•SYDNEY

First published in 2010 by Franklin Watts

Franklin Watts
338 Euston Road
London NW1 3BH

Franklin Watts Australia
Level 17/207 Kent Street
Sydney, NSW 2000

A CIP catalogue record for this book is available from the British Library.

Dewey number: 363.3'495

ISBN: 978 0 7496 9256 8

Franklin Watts is a division of Hachette Children's Books, an Hachette UK company.
www.hachette.co.uk

GRAPHIC NATURAL DISASTERS: EARTHQUAKES produced for Franklin Watts by
David West Children's Books, 7 Princeton Court, 55 Felsham Road,
London SW15 1AZ

Designed and produced by
David West Children's Books

Editor: Gail Bushnell

Photo credits:
p 45m, Matt Matthews

Printed in China

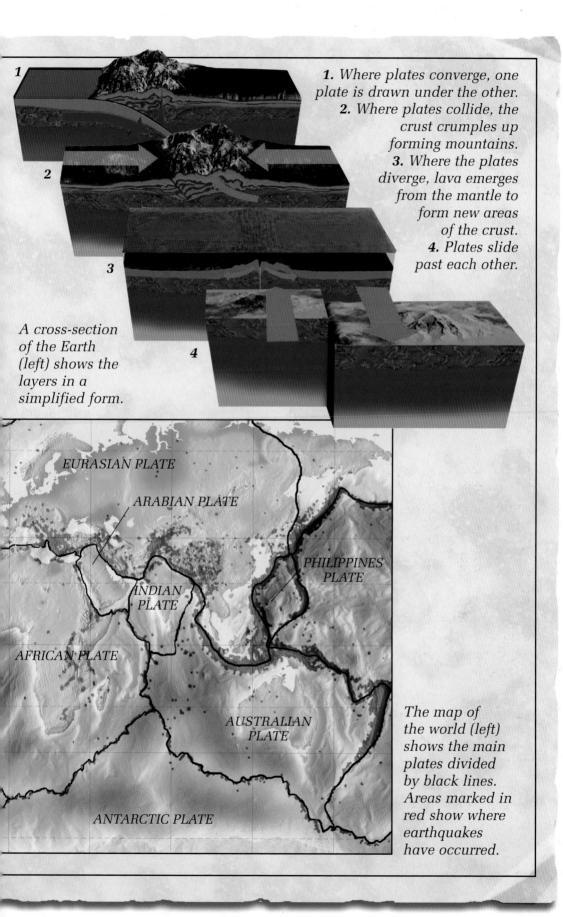

1. Where plates converge, one plate is drawn under the other.
2. Where plates collide, the crust crumples up forming mountains.
3. Where the plates diverge, lava emerges from the mantle to form new areas of the crust.
4. Plates slide past each other.

A cross-section of the Earth (left) shows the layers in a simplified form.

1

2

3

4

EURASIAN PLATE

ARABIAN PLATE

PHILIPPINES PLATE

INDIAN PLATE

AFRICAN PLATE

AUSTRALIAN PLATE

ANTARCTIC PLATE

The map of the world (left) shows the main plates divided by black lines. Areas marked in red show where earthquakes have occurred.

1. When plates move against each other they can become locked together due to friction. For a while they cannot move and energy builds up.

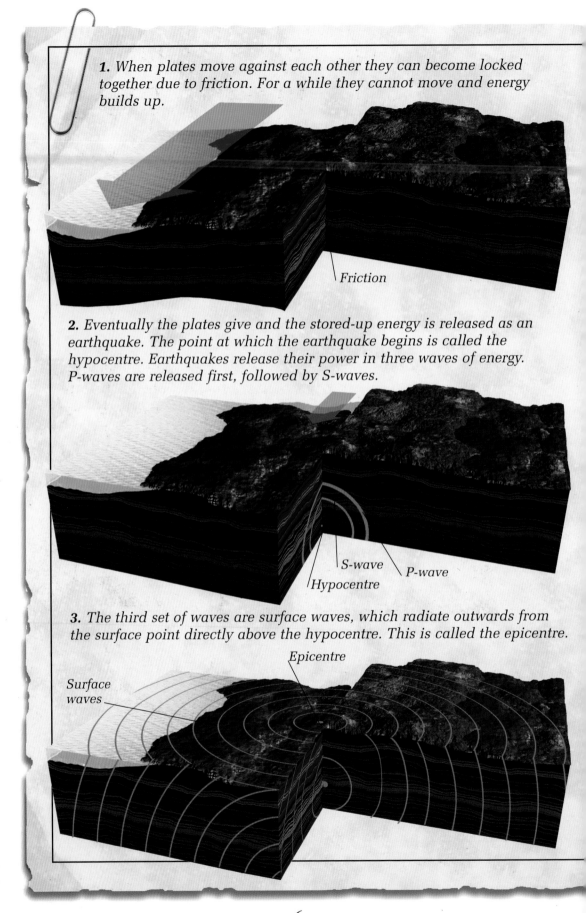

Friction

2. Eventually the plates give and the stored-up energy is released as an earthquake. The point at which the earthquake begins is called the hypocentre. Earthquakes release their power in three waves of energy. P-waves are released first, followed by S-waves.

S-wave   P-wave

Hypocentre

3. The third set of waves are surface waves, which radiate outwards from the surface point directly above the hypocentre. This is called the epicentre.

Epicentre

Surface waves

As Earth's plates slide against each other, occasionally they get stuck. When they eventually give the stored-up energy is released in a series of shock waves. This is known as an earthquake. It can be very mild, so that we don't even notice it or very violent, where surface structures – such as bridges and buildings – collapse!

WAVES

The first waves released from the hypocentre are primary, or P-waves, which can be felt as a sudden jolt. Secondary, or S-waves, arrive a few seconds later and are felt as a series of side-to-side tremors. Finally, surface waves are released. These can be either Rayleigh waves or Love waves. Both these surface waves can do great damage to surface structures such as buildings.

SURFACE WAVES
There are two types of surface wave. They each have their own special movement. Rayleigh waves create a rolling movement, which makes the land surface move up and down.

Rayleigh waves

Love waves

Love waves (named after the mathematician A.E.H. Love) make the ground shift from side to side.

SAN FRANCISCO, 1906

THE SAN FRANCISCO OF 1906 WAS AS FINE A CITY AS ANY IN AMERICA. SAN FRANCISCANS WERE PROUD OF IT.

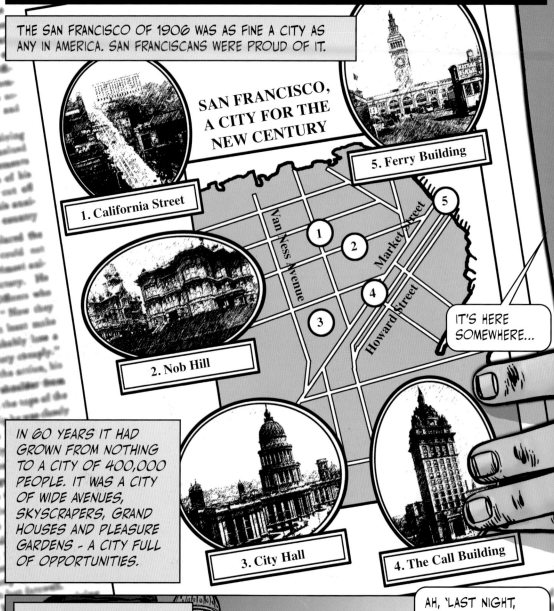

SAN FRANCISCO, A CITY FOR THE NEW CENTURY

1. California Street

2. Nob Hill

3. City Hall

4. The Call Building

5. Ferry Building

Van Ness Avenue

Market Street

Howard Street

IT'S HERE SOMEWHERE...

IN 60 YEARS IT HAD GROWN FROM NOTHING TO A CITY OF 400,000 PEOPLE. IT WAS A CITY OF WIDE AVENUES, SKYSCRAPERS, GRAND HOUSES AND PLEASURE GARDENS - A CITY FULL OF OPPORTUNITIES.

AT DAWN ON 18 APRIL, FRED HEWETT, A REPORTER ON 'THE ENQUIRER', AND TWO FRIENDS WERE DISCUSSING THE PREVIOUS EVENING'S GALA AT SAN FRANCISCO'S MISSION OPERA HOUSE.

AH, 'LAST NIGHT, WORLD FAMOUS ITALIAN TENOR ENRICO CARUSO GAVE A MARVELLOUS PERFORMANCE IN THE ROLE OF DON JOSÉ, IN BIZET'S OPERA 'CARMEN'.'

THE CITIZENS OF SAN FRANCISCO WERE USED TO EARTHQUAKES. MINOR RUMBLES WERE FREQUENT. THE CITY HAD BEEN BUILT ON A FAULT IN THE EARTH'S CRUST.

EVERY SO OFTEN, THE TWO SIDES OF THE FAULT WOULD SLIDE AGAINST EACH OTHER A LITTLE AND SAN FRANCISCO WOULD SHUDDER.

BUT THIS WAS DIFFERENT.

11

SOME PEOPLE STAYED IN THEIR HOUSES.

OTHERS RUSHED OUTSIDE...

...TO THEIR DEATHS.

THEN, ALMOST 30 SECONDS LATER, THE SHAKING STOPPED.

THE STREETS WERE FILLED WITH PEOPLE, MANY STILL IN THEIR PYJAMAS. THEY WERE TOO AFRAID TO RETURN TO THEIR HOMES.

MANY HOUSES HAD BEEN BADLY DAMAGED.

THE FIRST CONCERN OF FIREFIGHTERS AND SURVIVORS WAS FOR THE INJURED.

THAT SOON CHANGED.

BROKEN GAS PIPES, OVERTURNED STOVES AND CRACKED CHIMNEYS ALL PLAYED THEIR PART IN STARTING THE FIRST FIRES.

THIS ONE'S DRY TOO, CHIEF!

BUT WHEN THE FIREFIGHTERS WENT TO PUT OUT THE BLAZES...

THE WATER MAINS MUST ALL BE BROKEN.

THE INJURED WERE TAKEN TO THE MECHANICS' PAVILION, A LARGE EXHIBITION HALL, AS ALL THE HOSPITALS HAD CLOSED.

ARMS, LEGS, SKULLS, BACKS - I'VE HARDLY SEEN A BONE THAT'S NOT BEEN BROKEN!

THERE, AS GOOD AS NEW. NEXT ONE, NURSE.

MEANWHILE, AT THE COURTS OF JUSTICE, MAYOR EUSTACE SCHMITZ WAS HOLDING A MEETING. BY HIS SIDE WAS GENERAL FREDERICK FUNSTON. THE ARMY HAD ARRIVED IN THE CITY.

GENTLEMEN, THE FEDERAL TROOPS, THE MEMBERS OF THE REGULAR POLICE FORCE AND ALL SPECIAL POLICE OFFICERS...

...HAVE BEEN AUTHORISED BY ME TO KILL ANY AND ALL PERSONS FOUND ENGAGED IN LOOTING OR IN THE COMMISSION OF ANY OTHER CRIME.

NEARBY, AT THE US MINT, FRANK LEACH, THE SUPERINTENDENT, MET WITH LIEUTENANT ARMSTRONG.

ON THE ROOF OF THE MINT.

WE HAVE 60 MEN INCLUDING YOUR SOLDIERS, LIEUTENANT. WE HAVE OUR OWN WATER SUPPLY BUT THE ROOF IS OUR WEAKEST POINT.

THERE ARE FIRES IN FRONT AND BEHIND US. THEY'RE GOING TO MEET JUST ABOUT HERE. I HAVE TO BE READY FOR THEM.

I HAVE OVER 200 MILLION DOLLARS WORTH OF GOLD IN THE VAULTS, LIEUTENANT.

I'M NOT GOING TO GIVE UP THAT, OR THIS BUILDING, WITHOUT A FIGHT!

WITHOUT WATER THE FIRES WERE GETTING OUT OF CONTROL ALL OVER THE CITY. FIRE CHIEF CONLON HAD MANAGED TO GET SOME EXPLOSIVES.

WE NEED TO BRING DOWN BUILDINGS IN THE FIRE'S PATH TO MAKE A FIRE BREAK. THE MAYOR WILL ONLY LET US BLOW UP THE BUILDINGS ALREADY ON FIRE!

IT'S NO GOOD. WE NEED DYNAMITE. THE GUNPOWDER'S JUST SPREADING THE FIRE.

16

EARLIER IN THE DAY, LIEUTENANT FREDERICK FREEMAN, IN COMMAND OF THE USS PREBLE AND TWO FIREBOATS ARRIVED AT THE WATERFRONT.

FREEMAN TOOK THE FIREBOATS TO THE SOUTH END OF THE WATERFRONT.

FILL SOME BARRELS WITH FRESH WATER FOR THE REFUGEES.

THE FIREBOATS COULD PUMP SEA WATER ON TO THE FIRE.

AT NOON THE FIRE HAD REACHED THE MECHANICS' PAVILION.

GET THE WORST CASES TO THE WATERFRONT. THERE'S A HOSPITAL SHIP THERE.

17

THE WATERFRONT WAS CROWDED.

REFUGEES DESPERATE TO FLEE THE FIRE MINGLED WITH SIGHTSEERS FROM ACROSS THE BAY WHO WERE DESPERATE TO SEE IT.

BACK AT THE MINT, THE FIRE HAD SPREAD UP TO ITS WALLS.

LOOK! THE GLASS IS MELTING!

SUDDENLY...

THE COLLAPSING WALLS SENT A JET OF FLAMES INTO THE BUILDING...

...FOLLOWED BY CHOKING BLACK SMOKE.

BUT WHENEVER THE SMOKE CLEARED, THE MEN RUSHED BACK IN KEEPING THE WOODWORK FREE FROM THE FLAMES.

CINDERS RAINED DOWN ON THE ROOF.

BY 5:00 PM THE FIRE HAD MOVED ON. THE MINT WAS SAFE.

19

THAT FIRST NIGHT THE SKY GLOWED RED FROM THE BLAZE OF THE BURNING CITY.

AT THE FOOT OF HOWARD STREET, LIEUTENANT FREEMAN AND HIS MEN BATTLED ON.

BY 10:30 PM THEY HAD WON.

SINCE THE EVENING OF THE 19TH, LIEUTENANT FREEMAN AND HIS MEN HAD BEEN AT THE NORTH END OF THE WATERFRONT. THEY HAD MANAGED TO GET THEIR HOSES NEARLY TWO KILOMETRES INTO THE CITY.

LATER, ON THE WATERFRONT...

THE WIND IS BLOWING THE CINDERS TOWARDS THE WAREHOUSES!

THE TWO FIREBOATS SENT THEIR WATER JETS HIGH INTO THE AIR.

THE FINE SPRAY OF WATER QUENCHED THE BURNING CINDERS.

AT 3:00 AM THE WATERFRONT FIRE WAS UNDER CONTROL.

WEST OF THE WATERFRONT, THE FLAMES HAD BECOME ONE HUGE INFERNO. IT WAS MOVING WEST, NORTH OF MARKET STREET, AND THREATENED THE WHOLE CITY. ON THE 20TH, THE FIREFIGHTERS MADE A LAST STAND AT VAN NESS AVENUE.

BUILDINGS WEST OF VAN NESS AVENUE WERE BLOWN UP.

3,000 VOLUNTEERS HELPED THE FIREFIGHTERS TO MAKE SURE NO FLAMES CROSSED THE FIRE BREAK.

THE FIRE BREAK WORKED. AT 3:00 PM ON THE 21ST, THE FIRE STOPPED. IT HAD RUN OUT OF THINGS TO BURN. THE HEART OF THE CITY WAS A MASS OF BLACKENED RUINS.

24

WHAT THE EARTHQUAKE HAD STARTED THE FIRE HAD FINISHED. OVER SEVEN SQUARE KILOMETRES OF THE CITY HAD BEEN DESTROYED. NEARLY 3,000 PEOPLE LOST THEIR LIVES.

THANKS TO LIEUTENANT FREEMAN, RELIEF WAS ABLE TO POUR INTO THE WATERFRONT. THE HOMELESS WERE WELL CARED FOR.

REBUILDING STARTED ALMOST AT ONCE. THE MONEY IN THE MINT'S VAULTS HELPED TO GET THE FINANCIAL DISTRICT BACK ON ITS FEET. WITHIN A YEAR, THE FOUNDATIONS OF A NEW CITY HAD BEEN LAID.

THE END

KOBE, JAPAN
THE GREAT HANSHIN EARTHQUAKE, 1995

IT WAS 17 JANUARY 1995, JUST BEFORE DAWN, AT THE HOME OF KAZUO NAKAMURA.

KAZUO NAKAMURA LIVED IN ONE OF THE OLDER DISTRICTS OF KOBE.

KOBE'S NEWEST PARTS WERE OUT ON OSAKA BAY. TWO HUGE ARTIFICIAL ISLANDS SUPPORTED THE CRANES, DOCKS AND WAREHOUSES OF KOBE PORT.

KOBE WAS BUILT ON A THIN STRIP OF LAND. OSAKA BAY WAS TO THE SOUTH.

TO THE NORTH STOOD MOUNTAINS.

THREADING ITS WAY THROUGH THE CITY RAN THE HANSHIN EXPRESSWAY. THE TIME WAS STILL EARLY MORNING.

THE FIRST COMMUTERS OF THE DAY WERE ARRIVING AT DAIKAI SUBWAY STATION.

AT KOBE PORT, THE VIOLENT SHAKING TURNED THE GROUND TO QUICKSAND. CRACKS YAWNED OPEN, TEARING UP THE GROUND AS IF IT WERE PAPER.

ALONG A SECTION OF THE HANSHIN EXPRESSWAY...

...THE SUPPORT COLUMNS GAVE WAY.

ELSEWHERE ON THE EXPRESSWAY, YOSHIA FUKAMOTO FOUGHT TO CONTROL HIS BUS.

NO STRUCTURE WAS SAFE. THE SHAKING SEARCHED OUT WEAK SPOTS. A WALL HERE, A SUPPORT COLUMN THERE. SOMETIMES A COMPLETE FLOOR.

IN BUILDING AFTER BUILDING, THE UPPER STORIES DROPPED LIKE STONES ON TO THE LOWER ONES.

WHOLE FLOORS DISAPPEARED AS IF THEY HAD NEVER EXISTED.

AND THEN THE ROARING STOPPED. ON THE EXPRESSWAY, YOSHIA FUKAMOTO HELPED HIS PASSENGERS OFF THE BUS.

THEIR CITY HAD CHANGED FOREVER.

IN THE OLD PART OF KOBE, KAZUO NAKAMURA CRAWLED FROM UNDER HIS RUINED HOME.

HIS NEIGHBOURS' HOUSES LOOKED LIKE HIS OWN. ABOVE THE BROKEN SKYLINE HE COULD SEE THE GLOW OF FIRES AGAINST THE LIGHT OF DAWN.

OVER 5,000 PEOPLE LOST THEIR LIVES IN THE EARTHQUAKE. 500 MORE WOULD DIE IN THE FIRES THAT FOLLOWED. THE EARTHQUAKE HAD LASTED JUST 20 SECONDS. IT WOULD TAKE YEARS FOR KOBE TO BE REBUILT.

THE END

KASHMIR, PAKISTAN
THE SOUTH ASIA EARTHQUAKE, 2005

IT WAS SATURDAY, 8 OCTOBER...

GOOD MORNING, CLASS.

...AND THE START OF A NEW SCHOOL WEEK AT THE GARHI HABIBULLAH HIGH SCHOOL FOR GIRLS.

TURN TO PAGE 42 IN YOUR TEXT BOOKS PLEASE, GIRLS.

AS MISS YASUB BEGAN THE MORNING LESSON, MARIA HUSSAIN GAZED OUTSIDE.

MOST OF THE STUDENTS WERE ENJOYING SPORTS IN THE AUTUMN SUNSHINE.

GARHI HABIBULLAH WAS A SMALL TOWN IN PAKISTAN'S FAR NORTH. IT WAS HOME TO 10,000 PEOPLE.

MANY TINY VILLAGES WERE PERCHED IN THE HILLS AND MOUNTAINS.

32 KILOMETRES TO THE SOUTH LAY MUZAFFARABAD, THE CAPITAL CITY OF PAKISTAN-CONTROLLED KASHMIR.

IN GARHI HABIBULLAH, MARIA AND HER CLASSMATES WERE BUSY WITH THEIR SCHOOL WORK.

AT 8:50 AM...

...AN EARTHQUAKE HIT THE TOWN.

GARHI HABIBULLAH HAD BEEN 32 KILOMETRES FROM THE EARTHQUAKE'S EPICENTRE. THE LARGE TOWN OF BALAKOT HAD BEEN EVEN CLOSER. HARDLY A BUILDING REMAINED STANDING.

11,000 PEOPLE DIED IN MUZAFFARABAD, 19 KILOMETRES FROM THE EPICENTRE.

IN THE MOUNTAINS COUNTLESS VILLAGES HAD BEEN SHAKEN APART OR BURIED UNDER GIANT LANDSLIDES.

THE EARTHQUAKE HAD BEEN FELT IN KABUL IN AFGHANISTAN, 402 KILOMETRES AWAY.

DETECTING & PREDICTING

Every year more than 150,000 earthquakes are recorded around the world.

DETECTING EARTHQUAKES

Devices for detecting earthquakes have been around for thousands of years. The ancient Chinese had a device that could show the direction of an earthquake's origin. Equipment today is far more sophisticated. Seismometers can measure the up-and-down and side-to-side vibrations of an earthquake. The size of an earthquake is measured using the Richter magnitude scale (see page 46).

PREDICTING EARTHQUAKES

Despite many years of research, predicting earthquakes is still largely a matter of informed guesswork. Accurate, short-term predictions are the goal of today's scientists. Most of the research is centred around the 'Dilatancy Theory'. This is when a rock becomes stressed before an earthquake. When a rock is stressed it begins to expand (dilate) due to small cracks in the rock getting bigger. This happens halfway towards its breaking point. Measuring the effects on a rock that is stressed, such as its magnetic properties and effects on ground water pressure, could be the key to predicting an earthquake.

This ancient Chinese earthquake detector (below) was made more than 2,000 years ago. Tremors would move a pendulum inside the casing. Levers attached to the pendulum and dragons would make a ball drop from the mouth of a dragon into the frog below, showing the direction of the earthquake.

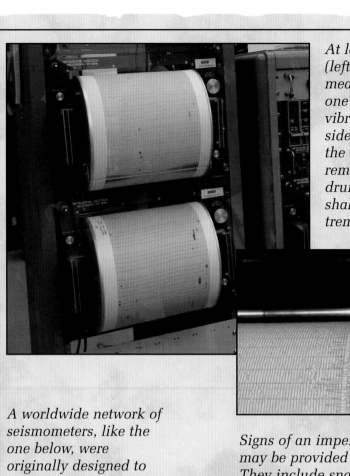

At least two seismometers (left) are needed to measure an earthquake – one for the up-and-down vibrations and one for the side-to-side vibrations. As the earth shakes, the pen remains still and the drum moves revealing shaky lines of the earth's tremor (below).

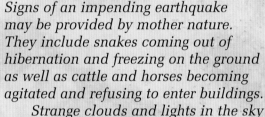

A worldwide network of seismometers, like the one below, were originally designed to monitor nuclear bomb testing. Now they provide valuable data on earthquake activity.

Signs of an impending earthquake may be provided by mother nature. They include snakes coming out of hibernation and freezing on the ground as well as cattle and horses becoming agitated and refusing to enter buildings. Strange clouds and lights in the sky are other strange occurrences reported before an earthquake.

GLOSSARY

cinders Small pieces of partly-burned, glowing wood.

commuters People who travel back and forth regularly, usually between a city and a suburb.

converge Move towards each other and eventually meet.

dilate To become wider or larger.

diverge Move away from each other.

dock A structure that is built out over water in a port where ships can moor to load or unload cargo.

fault A crack in the Earth's surface.

foreshock Small tremors that occur just before the main shock of an earthquake.

friction The resistance met by a surface of an object as it moves against another.

gala A special performance.

hibernation Period of time some animals spend during winter when their body systems slow down so that they go into a form of deep sleep.

lieutenant A middle-ranking officer in the navy.

magnitude The great size of something.

mechanic A person who repairs machines.

mint A place where new coins and banknotes are made.

pendulum A freely swinging rod with a weight at one end.

predicting Saying what will happen in the future.

refugee A person who has left his or her home, usually due to political or social unrest, to find a safer place to live.

seismometer A device that measures ground movement.

shudder To shake.

sophisticated Very complex.

stressed Under pressure or tension.

superintendent Person in charge of employees and their work.

timber Wood that is used for building.

THE RICHTER MAGNITUDE SCALE		
Magnitude	Earthquake Effects	Estimated Number Each Year
2.5 or less	Usually not felt, but can be recorded by seismograph.	900,000
2.5 to 5.4	Often felt, but only causes minor damage.	30,000
5.5 to 6.0	Slight damage to buildings and other structures.	500
6.1 to 6.9	May cause a lot of damage in very populated areas.	100
7.0 to 7.9	Major earthquake. Serious damage.	20
8.0 or greater	Great earthquake. Can totally destroy places near epicentre.	0.5

FOR MORE INFORMATION

ORGANISATIONS

British Geological Survey
Murchison House
West Mains Road
Edinburgh
EH9 3LA
Scotland
+44 131 667 1000
Email: ukegs@bgs.ac.uk
Website: http://earthquakes.bgs.ac.uk

FOR FURTHER READING

Blakes. *Earthquake* (Go Facts: Natural Disasters). London, England:
A & C Black, 2007.

Farndon, John. *Predicting Earthquakes*. Oxford, England:
Pearson Education, 2008.

Spilsbury, Richard and Louise. *Shattering Earthquakes* (Awesome
Forces of Nature). Heinemann Library, 2005.

Van Rose, Susanna. *Volcano & Earthquake* (DK Eyewitness Books).
London, England: Dorling Kindersley, 2008.

Watt, Fiona. *Earthquakes and Volcanoes*. London, England: Usborne
Books, 2007.

Watts, Claire and Trevor Day. *Natural Disasters* (Eyewitness Books).
London, England: Dorling Kindersley, 2006.

INDEX

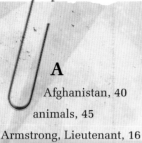